The Ultimate Ad

The Ultimate AdSense Bible

The Ultimate AdSense Bible

The Ultimate AdSense Bible:

Finally, Learn How To Master AdSense And Build

Super-Monetizing Sites!

by Mike Williams

Printed in the United States of America

The Ultimate AdSense Bible

Contents

Chapter 1: Introduction

You've probably heard a lot about Google AdSense (which is actually more accurately known as Google AdSense V1), but you may not know just what it is. Well, for one thing, it's a one of the hottest new ways to make money online without having to do a whole lot. If you've read Robert Kiyosaki's book, "Rich Dad, Poor Dad," you know that passive income is the best kind of income to have.

Passive income is income that you get without having to work for it. I know this may sound like some kind of "pie in the sky" get-rich-quick scheme, but passive income is for real. In fact, every single billionaire on earth uses the power of passive income to keep money coming in while he or she jets off to parties and resorts and such.

The best example of passive income in the physical world is real estate. When you own an apartment building and hire a property manager and a maintenance crew to take care of it for you and collect the rents, all you have to do is cash the checks that roll in.

Of course, passive income doesn't just happen overnight, or everyone would be getting it. In the case of the apartment building owner, it took money, time, and knowledge to set up an S corporation, find a building to buy, put up the cash to buy it with and get a loan for the rest, renovate it, then screen and hire the property manager and maintenance crew. But once that was all done, checks began rolling in with little or no effort.

Well, Google Adsense is the online equivalent of that. You'll have to invest just a little bit of time in learning about it, but once you get it set up you can look forward to seeing those nice checks roll in. Or, if you're totally online, seeing money flow into your PayPal account.

1.1 So Just What is Google AdSense?

Google AdSense is a fast and absolutely ridiculously easy way for people with websites of all types and sizes to put up and display relevant Google ads on the content pages of their site and earn money.

Because the Google AdSense ads relate to what your visitors came to your site to read about, or because the ads

11

match up to the interests and characteristics of the kind of people your content attracts, you now have a way to improve your content pages AND make some serious bucks off of them.

Google AdSense is also a way for site owners to provide Google search capability to visitors and to earn even more money by putting Google ads on the search results pages. Google AdSense gives you the ability to earn advertising revenue from every single page on your website—with a minimal investment of your time

So what kind of ads do you have to put up? That's the good part—you don't have to decide. Google does it for you. AdSense always delivers relevant ads that are precisely targeted—on a page-by-page basis—to the content that people find on your site. For example, if you have a page that tells the story of your pet fish, Google will send you ads for that site that are for pet stores, fish food, fish bowls, aquariums...you get the picture.

If you decide you want to add a Google search box to your site, then AdSense will deliver relevant ads targeted to the Google search results pages that your visitors' search request generated.

If you're into upgrades, Google is now offering "AdSense Premium", which is CPC based and, for the time being, offers less flexibility in terms of ad sizes -- only banners and skyscrapers are currently available. You can apply using existing AdWords accounts, or you can request a new account. Applicants are usually notified within a day as to whether they've been accepted for the program.

Here's the thing you need to know: Google has no strict criteria for acceptance into the AdSense program, and Ad Sense doesn't hit you with a minimum traffic requirement. The only criteria they're really sticky about is the standard "acceptable content" requirements, and that's pretty standard almost anywhere.

Google AdSense says they're serious about attracting quality content sites, and because of that they only allow AdSense members to serve one ad per page. This means you can't use AdSense for both banners and skyscrapers.(Note: banners are those horizontal ads that run up top and down bottom. Skyscrapers are the tall ads that run vertically, on the left and right of your page text.)

Once you've been accepted into Google AdSense, you'll be able to get the AdSense advertisements on any site you own using the same ad code, provided you obey the Google guidelines. (And that's very, very important—more on that later.)

Your reporting doesn't occur in real time, but is updated regularly throughout the day. Right now, you can't view reports based on a domain or site basis if you run the AdSense on more than one site.

Before you sign up, you really ought to read the lengthy and detailed FAQ on the AdSense site.

1.2 What Can it do for Me?

In three words, earn you money. More relevant ads on your pages translates into more clicks—and more money that you receive. Because when users click on an ad, Google will pay you. If you've set up your own sales team, you'll get an additional benefit: AdSense complements their efforts. It doesn't compete with them. With AdSense, you get a reporting page that gives you a breakdown on how your ads are doing and what they're bringing in.

Google has a huge advertiser base, so they have ads for all kinds of businesses and for just about every type of content no matter how broad or specialized it is. And since Google provides the ads, you don't have to spend time talking to your advertisers.

AdSense represents advertisers that span the spectrum. These advertisers range from large global brands to small and local companies. And ads are targeted by geography so global businesses can display local advertising easily. One more thing: you can use AdSense in many languages.

So how does AdSense figure out how to do all this targeted advertising? Well, AdSense has the ability to deliver relevant ads because the gurus at Google understand how web pages really work and they're continually refining their technology to make it smarter all the time.

For example, some words can have several different meanings depending on context. You've seen th is happen with "two" and "too" and "to." Google technology is smart enough to understand these distinctions from the context that the word appears in, so you get more targeted ads.

When you put a Google search box on your site you start making money off of web searches that people do on your site. This ability to search off of your page keeps them on your site longer—since they can search from right there where they are— and it will only take you a few minutes to get AdSense up and running. The best part, of course, is that AdSense is free for you to use.

1.3 What Kinds of Ads Will I Get on My Site?

Obviously, there are some kinds of ads you wouldn't want to have on your site, such as pornographic ones or ads for sleazy multi-level marketing schemes that scream "Make $30,000 a month just for watching TV!" in big red letters.

Well, you can put your mind at ease. Google has an ad review process that checks the ads they send to your site. This process ensures that the ads that you serve up are family-friendly and that they comply with Google's strict editorial guidelines.

Google's ad-screening team combines sensitive language filters, input from site owners like you, and a team of linguists with good old common sense to filter out ads that could be inappropriate for your content. And if that's not enough, you have to capability to block competitive ads and choose your own default ads. That's another nice feature: Google kind of lets you run your own show.

Now, another thing you might be concerned about is whether the ads will clash with the look, feel, and colors scheme you've got going with your site. Don't worry. You can customize the appearance of ads and choose from a wide range of colors and templates. Same thing goes for your search results page. And reports are customizable, too. Google provides flexible reporting tools that allow you to group your pages any which way you want.

That means you can view your results by URL, domain, ad type, category and more so that you can figure out where your earnings are coming from.

1.4   How do I Get Started?

It's easy to get started with AdSense and it only takes a few minutes. You fill out one single online application and that's it. Once you're approved, it takes only minutes to set up AdSense; all you have to do is copy and paste a designated block of HTML into the source code for your site. Once you do that, targeted ads will start showing up on your website.

To fill out the online application, go to:

https://www.google.com/adsense/application-1?apply=Click+Here+to+Apply/

1.5 Am I Going to Make a Lot of Money Off of This?

While we can't guarantee results, of course, since a lot of your success lies in your own hands, we wouldn't have written this book if we didn't believe in the power of Google AdSense. A lot of webmasters are making a lot of money off of AdSense, and there's no reason you shouldn't be one of them.

The amount of money you can make with Google AdSense mainly depends on what user needs your Website fills. For instance, a site about women's issues can make some serious bucks on AdSense because of the high level of competition for related keywords.

The CPC (cost per click) is the amount you get paid every time a user clicks on one of those ad banners. CPC rates for competitive keywords can be more than $1, which translates directly to your site's earning potential within the program.

However, if you're in a less competitive market, you'll make less money—that's just a fact of life. Still, it's unusual to see anyone using Google AdSense report earnings of less than an effective $1 CPM (cost per 1000 impressions), and the average runs in the range of $4-$5 CPM. Some people are making an effective CPM of $15 or more with AdSense. Oh, and best yet, this is all **after** Google takes its commission.

Commissions are definitely one thing is that's a little bit ambiguous with AdSense. Google doesn't publicize its "cut", and only displays the publisher's cut in proprietary member reports, so getting good, accurate information on this has been difficult.

To date, comparisons of AdWords rates with AdSense earnings add up to commissions of between 40% and 60%. People speculate all the time on user boards as to why Google refuses to publish its commission rates, but no one has the answer. It might have something to do with legal reasons or it could just be that Google wants to retain the ability to change rates without having to send out an announcement about it each time, which costs money.

Chapter 2: Building Content-Rich Sites

First off, why would you want to build content-rich websites? The short answer is "Because it keeps people on your site for awhile, it makes them come back, and they tell their friends about that site."

But why? Well, for one thing, people will stay on a content-rich site because it takes awhile to read an article or two. Thus, while they're reading the material, their peripheral vision (off to the sides) notices little ads that happen to surround that articles.

And if people start to realize that a certain site has good content that they like, and in particular, different content that constantly changes and is updated, then they'll check back to see what's new.

The worst thing in the world to have is a stagnant website that never changes. People will visit it exactly twice—the first time to check it out, and the second one to see what's changed—and when they find out it hasn't changed, they most likely won't come back. Ever.

2.1 What are Content-Rich Sites and Why Have One?

A content-rich site is one that has lots of informative articles up at it, usually centered around a theme. Most sites can't quite pull off being WikiPedia, so they specialize. For instance, you could do a site for dog owners. Possible articles on that site would cover:

- How to figure out what kind of dog you want
- Where to get a dog
- How to deal with a puppy
- Life stages of a dog
- House-training puppies
- Dog training
- What to feed dogs
- Whether to get more than one dog
- How to socialize dogs with other dogs and with cats
- Exercise needs of dogs
- Training dogs to do tricks
- Treating fleas
- Common dog ailments and when to go to the vet
- Dog nutrition
- Taking your dog on a trip

- Getting a pet sitter or boarding your dog if you don't take him on a trip

The articles you'll want to have on your site should be short enough so that someone can read them in about 5 minutes. This means you want to stick to articles of 250 to 750 words, with 300 to 600 words optimal. To give you an idea, a single page in a published novel has about 300 words.

Of course, your real purpose in putting up all these nice little short articles and changing them out frequently is not to just put information out into the world. It is to have a site that people will come back to so that they will see the Google AdSense ads, and click on them, and then you will get checks in the mail.

That's a key point, so I'm going to repeat it:

The purpose of having a content-rich website is to attract people to it, again and again, so that they will see the ads and click on them.

You might think it's lots of cool graphics and colors that make a site attractive to a visitor, but it's really the content. In order to make money from Google AdSense, you need to grasp that concept. Believe me, you could run a wonderful advertising campaign and develop all sorts of viral marketing tools and attractive affiliate programs.

29

But unless your Website is content-rich, the traffic spikes that you get for your efforts will only be temporary. The very best way to attract and retain an online audience is to provide content that's useful, valuable, informative, educational or just downright funny as hell or entertaining in some way.

2.2 *How Do I Build One?*

I know the notion of creating your very own content-rich website might be a little intimidating, but you can do it. It's not hard. You don't have to be a good write to have good content on your site. In fact, you don't have to be a writer at all. There are plenty of successful people who make a lot of money from Google AdSense and they don't write a word of that content. We'll talk more about that later, but you can hire writers, or have guest writers—it's not hard.

Anyone can create a content-rich Website by following a few key points:

- Have some discipline— maintain your site.
- Update that site often. Having a schedule is best.

- Be able to beg, borrow, or commission content

Discipline is key

To create a content-rich Website, you need to hone your focus and your self-discipline. I don't have to tell you how incredibly easy it is to waste hours, even days, just surfing around the web from one site to another. You can't let yourself get distracted like that or you won't accomplish anything. Start with setting a limit to surfing for fun so that you limit your searches to sites and resources that are relate very directly to your site's subject.

Discipline also applies to creating creation. Successful writers can't afford to wait for inspiration to strike before starting work. Instead, they develop a writing schedule for themselves and they stick with it like it was their job—since it is. As one famous writer said, "I write when I feel like it. And every morning at 9am, I make sure I feel like it." Schedule a time for yourself to sit down at your desk and write.

And you'll need to develop another schedule for when to add content to your Website, and follow that schedule religiously. Make a commitment to yourself and follow through with it.

And remember—if you just simply can't write, or you find yourself making too many excuses not to write content, just hire someone.

Go to Elance.com and post a project to write 20 articles of 300-600 words each for $5 to $10 each. You'll find someone.

Regular updates are critical to your site

Nothing is deader than a website that looks like somebody's forgotten about it. Regularly updating or modifying your site content gives you a big advantage over the competition. Web surfers will keep on coming back to your site if they notice that there's always something new to see, learn, or enjoy each time.

2.3 *What Kind of Content Should I Put Up?*

Any kind you want, of course, since we're talking about the internet. But seriously, you'll want to give this topic some consideration, since there's more interest in some topics than others.

You know the people who are your audience, since ideally you're talking about something you know about. For instance, if you're talking about Ultimate Frisbee, it's because you play it. So you know what other Ultimate people are like, and what they want to know and what they find entertaining.

Once you know that, you can decide about which types of content will best serve their needs and how to go about finding or creating it. Here are some general categories to get you started with your brainstorming:

- Editorials

- Feature articles

- Political opinion

- News stories

- Art galleries

- A conglomeration of the best content

- Reviews of movies, books, music

- Interviews

- Interactive features - polls, feedback, discussion groups, forums, chat

Editorials

Editorials are the opinion of someone who's seen as an expert in the field-- (either you or a guest contributor). This makes good content because people like to respond to it, either by agreeing with or opposing the writer. This can make for an exciting page, and you'll probably have to moderate it.

Give your people a way to make their views known; put up a bulletin board or guest book on your site. People will come back to read other responses to their comments. And you can use this feedback from your audience by incorporating it into a follow up article in the future.

For instance, is everybody complaining about a new government travel policy? Do an article on it, since clearly that's something people are talking about so they'll want to read about it.

Full-length Feature Articles

This is the most common and in many people's opinion one of the best forms of content. Depending on what your site is like, the articles could be long or brief, formal or chatty, technical or entertaining.

Here are some tips:

- Keep it short. While there aren't any hard and fast rules, you should keep these articles below 1200 words. If they are longer, make them into multi-part features. People hate to have to scroll down a lot.

- Articles should be relevant to your site.

- Articles ought to educate, entertain or inform. Don't overwhelm people; stick to one or two ideas.

- Refrain from rehashing an article you've read somewhere else. By publishing something that's new, you up the value and credibility of your site.

To Get Content

1. Offer to pay guest authors for their work. A guest author could be someone you found on your bulletin board who happens to write well.

2. Exchange articles with the guest author's site. Your site visitors benefit by providing them with another point of view. And you might just gain some new regular visitors from your guest author's site!

3. Make sure you get exclusivity. When someone writes for you, make sure they won't submit that same article to dozens of other Websites and newsletters. When your site publishes

exclusive content, you have opportunities for syndication in other publications, online and off, and you gain a lot of reader loyalty. The key phrase in a contract with a writer is that you're buying all rights, including electronic.

Can you use reprints?

Reprint articles written by others, but you must always obtain permission. All work, from the moment it is written, is copyright and owned by the author, whether it is marked with a copyright symbol or not. Content is not free. You can, however, make reprints interesting and personalized by putting your own 'spin' on the content. Write an introduction to the subject, or comment on the author's opinions or conclusions.

Take care to avoid 'editing' the original article without the author's permission. Avoid articles that have been reprinted many times before on other Websites and electronic publications.

Political Opinion

Using political opinion on your site can be tricky. People are deeply divided these days and have strong opinions. If you do run a political site, you'll probably want to carve out your own niche. Even then, be prepared for flamers from very different view points.

On the other hand, if you can manage to run a site that actually features a somewhat well-mannered debate, you'll have a huge hit on your hands. Be prepared to moderate this type of site.

News Stories

Your site can become a news source for the latest developments and happenings in certain niche area by providing timely news on topics of interest to your readers. I'm not saying you can be the next CNN or MS-NBC, because that takes building a huge operation. But what you can be is, for example, the CNN of the karate world, or the ABS-News of the bonsai tree hobbyists.

What you'll want to do is create a separate section of your site to deal with industry news. Or, devote an entire site to news updates. There are many ways of presenting news:

43

- As a feature article
- As short news clips, with a link to the full story
- As news stories, where each item is explained at length

However you decide present the news, make sure you give it your own personal style. Check out salon.com. Has its own style, doesn't it? Now look at drudgereport.com. That's another style. Make yours interesting, personal, chatty, fun, unique, or all of these – just make it **yours.**

Make sure your news is relevant, useful to your reader, and timely. Old news isn't no news at all, it's history! So how do you get news? By:

- Subscribe to ezines on your subject or topic
- Sign up for e-mail news delivery services
- Register to get regular press releases on your topic
- Surf the web for new news items
- Get news from newspapers, magazines and books
- Go to conferences, workshops or seminars and write about what you see and who you talk to

Conglomerating the best content

If you can make your site into the ultimate content resource on issues related to your topic, I guarantee you you'll attract and retain a loyal audience. Your site will become known as a The Place for anyone who wants information on your subject. For example, Harry Knowles has made aintitcoolnews.com into The Site for movie reviews and advance spoilers.

Since you're the expert on your topic, you can evaluate sites and other resources (ezines, directories, books, offline publications) and sniff out the best ones to list along with your rating and opinions.

This sort of content is like the old book reports you used to have to write for school. Read up thoroughly on your subjects, then hit the high points of a topic. Or, consider writing a summary of three separate article that have the same theme.

Reviews of movies, books, music

This is perhaps the easiest category to get content for. If you have friends who are movie, book, or music fans, they'll probably write reviews for free just for the thrill of seeing their stuff on a site.

Also, this is a never-ending source of content, since there are always new movies, books and music coming out. Contrast that with dog breeds—once you've written everything there is to say about every known breed, you have to wait for them to come up with a new breed!

If you want to have some fun, you can review movies yourself. And actually, if you're running your Google AdSense site as a business, you may even be able to deduct the cost of movie tickets from your taxes. Check with a tax consultant to make sure, though.

Music is easy, too, especially if you live in a town that has lots of live music or festivals. If not, you can buy used cd's online, listen, and review. In fact, you could even hire a high-school kid to do this, but check their writing skills first.

Books are a little harder, since they take more time to review and cost more than cd's and movie tickets. However, you can paraphrase what others have said if you're clever and don't violate copyright.

Interviews

This is a category you might want to get a freelance writer for. Go to elance.com and browse the profiles of Service Providers to see who does interviews, then talk to them. Many freelancers specialize in celebrity interviews, and that's what you want.

Interactive features - polls, feedback, discussion groups, forums, chat

This is one of the most popular types of sites for kids, teens, and young adults because they get to give their opinions (which many kids don't get to do enough of at home, according to them) and they get to talk to others.

So, if you want to run this kind of site, bear your target market in mind. It's worth paying a few bucks to a freelance writer or graphic artist to come up with fun games that are constantly changing, or new polls, since people will come back time and again to give their opinions. And don't forget surveys—people love to take surveys.

49

Chapter 3: SEO—Search Engine Optimization

You've probably heard of SEO, since it's very hot right now. It stands for Search Engine Optimization. SEO is the process of increasing the amount of visitors to a site by designing the site content so that the site ranks high in the search results of a search engine.

The higher a Web site ranks in the results of a search, the greater the chance that a user will visit that site. Let's face it, most people are lazy. They're not going to spend time clicking and scanning tons of pages of search results. Therefore, where a site ranks in a web search is absolutely critical for directing more traffic toward the site. SEO helps to make sure that a site is accessible to a search engine and improves

51

the chances that the site will be found by the search engine.

To understand how this works, you need to know a little bit about how search engines work. Typically, a search engine sends out a spider to fetch as many documents as it can. Then another program, called an indexer, reads these documents and makes an index based on the words each document contains. Each search engine uses a unique proprietary algorithm to create indexes so that hopefully only meaningful results are returned for each query.

These indexers compute the keyword density.

Keyword density refers to the how often a certain word appears in a given document. It's given as a percentage. Let's say you have a site about running shoes. A keyword density of 7% on "running" on that web page means that out of 1000 words, 70 of them are "running."

Unfortunately, the quick-buck con artists have figured this out, and they will put up a site that has a front page that is totally littered with keywords. To give you an idea, a normal key word density for the main key words is about 3 to 7%. What these people will do is have something insane like a 25% keyword density on their front page. Then that page ranks #1 in search engine results when users search for that word. Once the user is on the entry page, they're likely to enter the site.

Pornographers do this by putting up sites that have content like:

Sex, sex, sex. Sex is here. You want sex. We have sex. Pix of sex, lots of sex.

See how annoying that gets?

Search engines used to use meta-tags to search for web sites. This was nice, since the meta-tag was a hidden area of your page where you could put all the relevant keywords and not have to worry about making your content sound awkward by overusing certain words.

3.1 Things to Consider

There are many things to consider when you go to put keywords in the text of your pages. Most search engines index the full text of each page, so you should put your keywords throughout your text.

However, each search engine uses different ranking algorithms. And that's the really hard part--difficult though it may be, you need to keep all of them in mind.

General rules

Your main page should be full of keywords because that page has a higher chance of being indexed than other pages. And for some search engines, it will be the **only** page that is indexed.

Some engines will rank your page highly if it has at least 100 words on it, so consider that your minimum. Directories include pages based on the quality of their content, so make sure your pages aren't just lists of keywords. If you do that, you risk not getting in the big directories AND you will irritate readers—they won't come back.

<u>Important design concepts</u>

When you create your pages' content, pay attention to:

- Keyword prominence
- Proximity
- Density
- Frequency

The thing about keyword prominence is that the best place to place keywords in your text is at the top of each page, preferably the main page. The closer your keywords appear to the start of the page or the start of a sentence, the better. You'll frequently see "keyword prominence" used to describe search engines' algorithms. Be aware that some engines also say the bottom of the page should contain keywords as well.

It gets more complicated. Search engines view pages differently than people do.

Chrome. We're all about chrome. Chrome bumpers, chrome trinkets, we love chrome.

Now, you may think you did pretty good by putting your keyword, which was obviously "chrome", at the top of your page. A search engine, however, sees your page this way:

Home About Us Products Contact **Chrome** we're all about **chrome** **Chrome** bumpers **chrome** trinkets we love **chrome**

Now your keyword placement doesn't look nearly as good as it did before, does it? So the moral of the story is: try to put keyword-rich text at the very top of your page. If you put images at the top of your page, make sure to include ALT tags so the search engine ignores them.

Now, about keyword proximity. Some engines, such as Google, use keyword proximity as part of their ranking formulas. So what's it mean? Keyword proximity refers to how close keywords are to each other. You want to put your keywords as close together as possible and make sure your sentences are clear.

Here's an example:

Meow Mix sells the very best **cat**

food *as far as taste tests of actual cats are* *concerned.*

versus

Meow Mix scored number one in *taste tests to see what kind of **food** is* *really preferred by the typical **cat**.*

The two keywords are "*cat*" and "*food*." If a user searches for "*cat food*," the first sentence will rank higher because its keywords are closer to each other. Why do search engines do this? Because if you're searching for "running shoes", a page that contains "running shoes" is probably relevant, but a page that contains, "I was running late for work and forgot to put on my good shoes," probably is not.

Why is keyword density important? Because, as I said earlier, it measures how often that particular word comes up. Keyword density is also known as keyword weight. The higher the percentage of keywords in relationship to other text, the higher your page will rank—to point. Many search engines, Google included, have gotten wise to the fact that extremely high keyword densities are probably contrived.

Here's an example of how keyword density it measured. Let's assume the keyword phrase is "*cat food*."

Cat food *is our only business.*

Since "*is*", "*our,*" and other stop words are usually not counted, there are three "words" in the sentence: "*puppy food,*" (which the search engine counts as one word, since that's what it's searching for), *"only," and "business." "Cat food"* composes 1/3 of the sentence, or 33%.

Realistically, keyword density is almost never this high, nor should it be or your copy will sound very contrived. The recommended density is 3-7%. This means that your keyword should repeat 3-7 times for every 100 words.

Sure, that may not sound hard, but believe me--having 10 keywords and trying to repeat each one 3-7 times per 100 words of text is practically impossible. Instead of trying to do that (and having copy that sounds really weird), pick two or three of your most important keywords and try to use them 3-7 times for every 100 words.

So what about keyword frequency? Keyword frequency is a measure of the number of times keywords occur within a page's text. It's kind of related to the concept of keyword density. The thinking is that search engines want to see a word used more than once to make sure it's something you're really talking about. The best number of times to repeat a key word is 3-7 times.

Don't get overly clever and try to use tiny or invisible text to put keywords at the beginning of your pages. Search engines look for this, and when they find it they call it spam and they'll probably reject your site for it.

So, in a nutshell, you want to:

- Include at least 100 words in page text
- Use keywords at the beginning of the page
- Place keywords close to each other

- Repeat keywords 3-7 times for every 100 words

3.2 Likes and dislikes of Googlebots

What's a Googlebot? It's one of the little web-searching spiders (automated) that I talked about in the last section. And these spiders have definite preferences, so you want to make sure your content is good spider food.

Spiders like:

- Neat code—less lines of code than lines of text (or more lines of text than lines of codes.)

- Normal keyword densities of 3-7%.

- Lots of backlinks on pages that link back to your home page. (Top sites have an average of 300 backlinks.)

- Original content not found anywhere else.

- Quick downloads of sites, which means not a lot of dynamic URLS to other sites.

- Site maps.

- ALT Tabs for images.

- Link partners who are contextually relevant to your page (i.e., if your page is about buying real estate, links might about be how to get loans, how to prospect for deals, how to start a corporation...but not about pet gerbils, latest fashions, or cell phones.)

- New content every time the spider comes to check up on your site.

Spiders do not like:

- More lines of code than text.

- Nested tables.

- Super-high keyword densities, which they call "keyword stuffing".

- "Doorway pages" that act as a portal and which just happen to have super-high keyword densities.

- Too many backlinks to your home page from within your domain.

- Duplicate content from another site—regardless of who stole what from whom.

- Lots of dynamic URLs that cause a site to take forever to download.

- Repeating the exact same words in your linking text, which the spider will interpret as automated link swapping. (Interestingly, it's fine for the spiders to be fully automated, but they hate it when **we** do that!)

- Stale content that never changes.

Chapter 4: About Specific Keyword Density Ranges

With the decline of meta-tags, keyword density ranges have become very important. They've also become very controversial. Here's the thing: you want a high enough keyword density—at least 7%--that your keywords rank highly in the bigger search engines, such as Google, Yahoo, DogPile, and HotBot.

But, as we discussed, you don't want your keyword densities so high that they turn your content into over-hyped gobbledygook, nor do you want to raise a red flag when the spiders come crawling over your content. If your keyword density is 20% or more, the search engine will most likely red-flag you for "keyword stuffing" and penalize you by moving you down in the search results.

Thus, keyword density ranges are controversial. To make things worse, different search engines have different algorithms. One of them might thing an SEO keyword density of 18% is fine, another may not.

The only way a search engine can figure out just what your page is about is to search for the keywords you use. Those keywords don't necessarily have to be right there on the page—they can be in the title and in links that will lead to the page. Having said that, though, keywords that appear on your page are certainly the most common way that search engines use to decide what your page is all about. Keyword density refers to the ratio of keywords to the total number of words on the page.

Now I want you to look again at the paragraph above. There are 95 words total, and I used the word "keywords" exactly five times. The keyword ratio for the paragraph, then, is 5 divided by 95 times 100, or about 5.26%. Easy math, correct? You bet.

But how much does that stuff matter?

Well, it's not a matter of life and death, but it's pretty important. You see, when a search engine compares two pages to figure out which one ought to rank higher, keyword density will factor into it— usually pretty significantly. In fact, all other factors being equal (which is pretty much impossible, but let's pretend), the page with the higher keyword density will generally rank higher.

However, simple as Keyword Density is, it can also get really complex in a hurry. Do plurals or other stemmed variations of your keyword count as keywords? Should stop words, which are those common words you see all the time like "a" or "the," be ignored when calculating density?

Should you include off-page content, like meta tags and titles, in your calculations? What about keyword frequency or keyword proximity or keyword prominence? And like I've said before, bear in mind that if your keyword density gets too high, search engines just might realize it and penalize your page.

But now, hold on. Even though

keyword densities are getting to be a complex science with lots of complicated algorithms, you can do it!

Keyword densities really are not rocket science, so don't fall into the trap of making things more complicated than they need to be. Go to Google and search on "keyword density." The first three pages should be ones that provide about 20 or 25 different tools for calculating KWD.

Now all you have to do is pick one that feels user-friendly to you and use it to optimize your web page, noting the results. Now try something else: run a Google search on your keyword, and run the analysis on the first ten sites. Take a good hard look at the results. From this, you should get a good idea how your page will compare with the ten top ranking pages in

Google, at least in terms of keyword density.

Here's the thing that frustrates people, though: if you go and do that with three or four different KWD tools, you will no doubt come up with different numbers, but the graph of those numbers will look very similar. Don't worry about it, because the numbers aren't the most important thing. You only care how they compare to each other.

Something else you'll probably discover is that keyword density is not a very good indicator of rank. The top ranking page may have a much lower density than the page at number ten, for example.

Why does this happen, when you work so hard to get your keyword density high? It happens because KWD is only one factor among many. It's important to a good ranking, but it's not the be-all and end-all of a good ranking. What you really want to know from your analysis is the range of density values that rank well. Chances are good that if your page is below that range, getting on page one to compete with the big dogs will be tough, and if you're above that range, the search engines may think you're "keyword stuffing" and you'll be penalized. Just remember, though, the numbers are guidelines you should know, not carved-in-stone rules that forever define your fate. Experiment!

You may hear self-proclaimed website gurus say that keyword density should always run between two and eight percent or whatever the current numbers being quoted in forums across the Internet happen to be. That's partly true. Those numbers are probably fairly accurate for most keywords. They're based on averages and it's always good to stick close to an average.

But there's a problem. Here's how the problem goes: the most commonly used letter in English is the letter "E." If you wrote a ten word sentence, it would be much easier to use the letter E five times in that sentence than it would be to use, say, the letter Z five times. Letters aren't an even distribution. Neither are keyword. Big shock, huh?

Remember what I said earlier about not sounding awkward in your content? Well, the biggest thing about keyword density is that it must read well and sound very natural to a user. It's useless to get a page one ranking if your content is very lame.

Like the letter E, some keywords are easy to use a lot of while still sounding natural. For instance, if your keyword was "grass" on a site about lawn care, it wouldn't be hard to use "grass" a lot.

But some keywords just don't lend themselves to being used a lot—like "quince." (It's a type of fruit.) Here's the choice to be made: you can use an average range, which will work well most times, or you can spend time analyzing the top ten pages to find the best range for that particular keyword and be sure you're not trying to optimize for a Z or a quince.

Frustrated? Don't be! It isn't that hard. If you're still confused, check out a competitor's page in Google's cache (which highlights the keywords for you) to get a good visual feel for density.

Another good tip is to perform a "real person sanity check" on your content. Reading your optimized content out loud several times, and try to get a natural flow that will make the copy draw users who will come back. Then take a hard look at your content. If you can substitute a keyword for a pronoun without loosing your flow, do it.

For instance, if your keyword is "hammock", instead of a sentence saying, "I love to lie in it," say, "I love to lie in my hammock."

4.1 Do-it-Yourself SEO

There are a ton of free online SEO tools available on the internet. Most feature some very impressive statistics and information to help you optimize your website, analyze search engine positions, research your competitors, and lots of other things.

There are two ways you can use these free online SEO tools:

(1) If you're new to SEO, these tools provide excellent insight on how a website is performing and ranking. Use them to highlight issues and trends with your website and provide indicators for where

optimization work is
necessary.

(2) If you've had some
experience with SEO, these
tools will act as a
complement to the more
specialized SEO tools, like
WebPosition Gold or
SpyderOpts. You can also use
them to supplement an SEO's
internal knowledge base and
experience.

Here are some choice tools for both
new SEO users and more experience SEO
users:

Keyword Research Tool
http://www.webmaster-

toolkit.com/keyword-research-tool.shtml/
Use this to research appropriate words and
phrases to include in your webpage's body
text so that you'll rank higher. It's easy to
use. You just enter the word or phrase you
want to be found under, then the tool
suggests additional words and phrases for
you to consider using. You also have the
option to select from a range of top search
engines, e.g. Google, Yahoo, MSN, Teoma,
etc.

Keyword Analyser Tool
http://www.webmaster-
toolkit.com/keyword-analysis
This one will read the body of the page and
give you a report on what words are used
and how many times they are used.
Since most engines rank sites depending

on that site's keyword density (which typically ranges between 3% and 9%), this is a really good tool to have.

Search Engine Position Checker Tool
http://www.webmaster-toolkit.com/search-engine
This tool checks to see if your website appears in the first fifty results in major search engines for your designated keyword or phrase. If your URL is present, the tool outputs what position it occupies. This tool also lets you know if any other URLs from your domain appear in the search results.

Link Popularity Tool
http://www.instantposition.com/link_pop
ularity_check.cfm

This tool will measure the total number of links or "votes" that a search engine finds for your website. One of the best feature is that besides tabulating data, it also produces a very cool graph of the resulting data. One other nice feature is the ability to compare your website to your competitors to help you with your overall marketing strategy.

Meta Tag Generator
http://www.webmaster-toolkit.com/meta-tag
This automatically generates a Meta Keyword tag by reading the page you specify, removing common words from it, and picking the most used words on the page. Extra weight is given to words in a heading tag (etc.)

Search Term Suggestion Tool

http://inventory.overture.com/d/searchin
ventory/suggestion/

This one tells you how many times a
certain keyword was searched for at
Overture.com. It will also show all related
searches for that keyword. It's a good thing
to use to determine search frequency
among related keyword phrases

Search Engine Optimization Tool

http://www.instantposition.com/seo_doct
or.cfm

This is a tool with a lot of power. It tests
the performance of a web site by analyzing
a page by important criteria such as title
and content. Then it ranks the page against
the criteria that the top search engines use.

And as if that isn't enough, it also provides SEO advice to improve your overall ranking. The report it puts out is well laid out and easy to read.

The Ultimate AdSense Bible

Chapter 5: About Extreme Content Sites

What is extreme content? Don't worry—it's not adult content, or graphic violence, or even anything terribly controversial. "Extreme content" refers to very large sites ranging in size from 1,000 to 10,000...even 300,000 pages.

Now why on earth would anyone go to the trouble to create anything that huge, other than trying to get into the Guinness Book of World Records? They do it in order to have a ton of pages that will result in a massive saturation upon the search engines.

Let's look at it this way: say you've got a nice little ten-page site. Those ten pages give you ten chances to get listed somewhere in a search engine's rankings.

Contrast that with an extreme content site of 1,000 pages. That site has 1,000 chances of getting listed in the rankings, which means some of their pages will no doubt get listed up near the very top.

Of course, not all of the 1,000 pages will rank in the top 10—there's not room, by definition—but you've got a better chance that some of them will. And when you get all that traffic streaming into your site, you can direct them to your main site by using pop-unders or links and articles on those pages.

Of course, you can also use them to make big bucks by putting Google ads on these pages using Google AdSense.

However, keeping track of thousands of pages requires a good organizational scheme. You'll want to use a service like Wordtracker.com or the Overture keyword tool to find out the most popular keywords. Once you've figured those out, use a tool like traffichurricane.com to build a huge site.

So what all do you put in an extreme content site?

- Articles – be sure and organize them by categories. Otherwise, it'll be like trying to find a needle in a haystack. And it's critical that they be SEO keyword-rich.

- Web forums – people love forums where they can discuss things, so give them a place to vent and have their little flame wars.

- Polls – people also love to be asked their opinions, so give them a place to express it, even if it's just a multiple-choice poll.
- Games – a huge number of people love to play games.

So what sort of strategy do you use to create an extreme content site? Well, for one thing, you don't try to do it at once. Having said that, though, if you think you want to go extreme, make sure you set up a basic structure that allows for expansion.

Start small, but leave room to grow. For instance, start out with a ten-page site that stays on one topic. Then, once you get Google AdSense going and the checks are coming in, use the tools discussed in this book to determine the hottest keywords of the month and use the other tools we talk about to build your keyword-rich content.

Before you know it, you'll be up to thirty, sixty, even a hundred pages. Then you'll just need to make a commitment to add a certain number of pages each month.

So now that you've got the gameplan, get going!

Another great way to build a quick content site is with other peoples articles using a tool like Article Site Builder.

This tool builds content pages by pulling articles from article site directories like ArticleCity.com and EzineArticles.com

The Ultimate AdSense Bible

Chapter 6: Using Traffic Equalizer

Traffic Equalizer (http://TrafficEqualizer.com) is a hot tool that many site developers use to massively increase traffic to their site and thus put them on a level playing field with the big boys. TR boasts that they drive highly targeted buyers to your site.

In a nutshell, you import a list of keywords, you fill in a few form fields, and the program automatically creates optimized pages. They claim it's very search-engine friendly. It is a program that quickly generates hundreds or thousands of pages that are specially designed to rank well on search engines for huge lists of keyword phrases. You've probably seen these types of pages before. They feature an ad on top and then there are listings that look like a directory or a search engine.

All you have to do is make a list of keywords, type them into Traffic Equalizer and the software crawls search engine data to bring back the top results for that keyword. Then it lists those sites and inserts your site at the top...and voila! It creates pages that are supposedly designed to rank well for search engines.

The thing is, some of the pages it produces can look a bit clunky, like this:

6.1 Using Traffic Equalizer

The Ultimate AdSense Bible

You should always put Traffic Equalizer pages on a separate domain, on a separate IP, even on a separate server. Keep it as far away from your website as possible. More on why later.

Traffic Equalizer provides a template that's...well, not great-looking. And here's the thing: many users are saying that when they use that original template, unmodified, their pages and in some cases their entire website are getting dropped from Google's index. The work-around here is for you to create a new template, with your own graphics. Change the colors and add some of your own new text. You want to change this from being easily recognizable to Google.

Traffic Equalizer runs a support forum...for product owners. So if you get

TE, be sure you take full advantage of it to get tips and such. Mind you, in those forums you'll see posts from users who've gotten banned from search engines. What you want to do is look for people who are getting tons of traffic from Traffic Equalizer and find out their secrets.

There are also some helpful sites, such as http://www.webtrafficstrategies.net/cb_te mplates which offer different templates for TE.

Here's a sample of what they offer:

6.2 *Google's Guidelines*

I wouldn't be doing my job right if I didn't caution you that using TE could get you thrown out of Google, and the AdSense program.   That's why I've listed some cautions above. Here's what Google has to say about it in their guidelines:

"Avoid tricks intended to improve search engine rankings. A good rule of thumb is whether you'd feel comfortable explaining what you've done to a website that competes with you. Another useful test is to ask, "Does this help my users? Would I do this if search engines didn't exist?"

The Ultimate AdSense Bible

Chapter 7: Using Traffic Hurricane

Traffic Hurricane (TH) is a little bit interesting in the way it's marketed. It is only sold through its JV Partners links. If you go to http://www.traffichurricane.com, you will see this:

However, you can solve that little problem by going directly to one of the free download pages of one of the Traffic Hurricane Site Resellers.

With this free version you can build tens of thousands of web pages very quickly. The downside is that with the free version you will be showing ads on your pages that belong to the reseller of the copy of Traffic Hurricane you downloaded.

The upside is you can try this new version of TH and if you like it you can upgrade and remove these ads or make them your own.

For the cost I can not recommend this product highly enough! It is worth its weight in gold!

TH is much-loved by many site owners, who describe it as "the perfect spider food." They also love that it works very well for Google AdSense. TH has much in common with TE. They're both not just doorway page creators. This is good, because doorway pages get banned from the search engines and Google, in particular, is very averse to them. TH users like the unique content and linking structure of TH, and they most especially love that the search engines love it.

TH creates literally thousands of laser targeted pages so fast you won't believe it. It combines that ability with a user-friendly interface that takes minimal effort on your part. Basically, it does what developers used to have to do by hand—TH automates it.

As a result, users can create pages much faster and thus receive many thousand more targeted hits every day. They claim they use "Top Quality Content" on all the pages it creates—whatever that means. It probably means they're trying to address TE's shortcomings of crummy content.

Their marketing literature says, "Our system is not just creating a bunch of keyword rich pages that are going to automatically forward the traffic that arrives at them to your main web or affiliate link. They will actually provide good quality content that will not be banned by search engines."

TH includes the ability to add RSS feeds for dynamic up to date content. What are RSS feeds? They are content taken from other information service web pages and inserted into your web pages automatically.

Search engines love this type of content because every time a search engine spider visits your site, there's always some new content. Traffic Hurricane Pages are also fully customizable. Like I mentioned in the last chapter, one of the big reasons most of the pages that TE creates get banned in a hurry by the major search engines is that they all look and act the same.

Traffic hurricane pages are fully customizable as far as the amount and type of content placed on them. Thus, there's a better chance that TH pages will be unique. There are 14 templates to choose from and you can pick from a huge range of colors and add up to 3 images on each of the pages that will be created to ensure that your pages will be unique. If you have a special logo that you've designed, this would be the place to use it.

The Ultimate AdSense Bible

Chapter 8: MetaWebs

MetaWebs has been called the Cadillac of search engine optimization/traffic builder sites. Metawebs is a server-based software which allows you to create unlimited search engine optimized web pages. And business has been good. Business has been so good for them that MetaWebs (MW) (http://www.metawebs.com/) has recently been a victim of its own success. In June of 2005, they closed down temporarily after having sold out their third level of membership. They say they will offer a higher level of membership to this popular tool.

Messages posted to user boards state that the old Tier 3 price was $500 down and $500 per month, and that the new tier will cost approximately $10,000. Clearly, MW is a power tool designed for serious users who truly want to maximize income.

How is MW able to charge such high prices, prices people are lining up to pay? Well, because MW is a software release from SEO "expert" Nathan Anderson. The big claim is that MW is "The First White Hat Software Tool". The program is supposedly able to "(generate) non-foot-printable, traffic-generating-websites the search engines absolutely love..."

Users were understandably skeptical of these bold claims at first, and skittish of the high price of MW.

The buzz that MW has tried to

create is that TE, TH and the rest are just black-hat spam machines that create content that's mediocre at best.

Anderson claims that while MW sounds like a doorway page generator, his product is different because unlike doorway pages, "MetaWebs are likely to be bookmarked and revisited because of their valuable content." Meaning his product creates pages with actual content while doorway page generators just produce pages designed to trick search engines.

I talked about doorway pages earlier. Now let me give you a definition. As defined by About.com, doorway pages are "pages designed to be visible only by search engine spiders, and usually just have blobs of keywords all over them."

MetaWebs, on the other hand,

creates websites that are highly optimized, formatted in php templates, and filled with live, active content from Anderson's Meta search engine.

When MW was released, its connotation as a White Hat software tool was met with disbelief and disdain by many users who just didn't want to believe. Their main criticism had to do with the potential for spam to ruin search engine results. A whole lot of users feel that SERPs (Search Engine Results Pages) have become way overcrowded with spam sites and doorway pages which they view as the bane of their existence. Others blame MetaWeb for the increase in search engine spam.

The question is being asked on forums, "How long will it be before

Google's AdSense team starts cracking down on AdSense accounts that are used on pages generated from keyword tools like this?" Apparently, users who do things by hand are irked by those who use automated tools, and there is justification for this.

There is also the fear that eventually, someone will—if they haven't already—use MW for is spam. And when that happens, everyone using MW will suffer, since MW will leave the tracks necessary for Google to eventually detect the machine generation, and then those pages or sites will be dropped."

Others say that MetaWebs has no business being called "white hat" because it is an automation tool and that, because of the misuse, software generated pages ought to be considered a black hat technique.

Anderson disputes this. He admits MetaWebs does indeed have the potential to produce spam pages, but that's not his fault. It's the fault of people who misuse his product. It can be misused, he says, "...Especially if people don't customize the pages that MetaWebs spits out. But if they think of MW as a site-building tool, instead of a spam page machine, they should never have a problem."

He's right. Any tool that humans use, from tire irons to golf clubs to guns, can be misused. It's all about intent. And my opinion is that a power web tool like MW shouldn't be penalized or banned from SERPs just because some people misuse it. That's like saying we should ban cars because a few people every year misuse them to run over others.

It's up to the user as to how they use MW. You could churn out pages using the advanced tools in Dreamweaver if you wanted to. That doesn't mean that Dreamweaver is bad software. Anderson feels that he is "empowering the masses with something that circumvents the SEO."

The Ultimate AdSense Bible

Chapter 9: Additional Web Page Creation Software

If you're skittish of what TE and TH create and MetaWebs just isn't in your budget, here are a few other options. These tools don't break the search engines' SEO rules as long as you use them right.

In a larger sense, this advice applies to most any content creation tool. You can use those tools in an honest and ethical way—which is what we recommend—to create very interesting and compelling content, or you can use them in an unethical way to lure users to a site that turns out to be not what they thought it was.

Even though the latter approach will draw more traffic, we don't recommend it.

And not just because it's wrong, either. Think about it: if you went to a site and it wasn't what it had claimed to be, you'd suspect the site owner cheated the search engines. And then you wouldn't stick around long enough to click on any of the ads, would you?

Nope, neither would we. It's called "backlash."

And now, on to the wonderful tools that represent some of our top picks for compelling keyword-rich content creation.

9.1 Directory Generator

113

As the name implies, Directory Generator DirectoryGenerator.com works on directories, also know as portals. The creator of DG noticed that many of these directories and portals have been quietly driving thousands upon thousands of visitors to their own sites on a daily basis year after year.

To appreciate how DG works, you have to know a bit about directories—there are two types.

1. General Directory - A General Directory contains listings of just about anything on the planet. It is not targeted in any way, shape or form.

2. Specific Niche Directory - These directories are vertical

in nature and they focus on just one industry or topic. Everything on this type of site is about one topic, so it's all very relevant.

DG focuses on the specific niche directory. However, it wasn't easy. Creating a directory has always been a tough job: time consuming, complicated, and frustrating. The big online directories contain thousands of links and resources which can take a live person thousands of hours to create. If one person did it, it would take years. But DG's found a way to automate the process.

Some of their features include:

- Photo Shots of Websites - Each resource Directory Generator creates contains a Photo Shot of the Website itself. This gives users a preview of the website before you look at it.

- RSS Equalizer Integration - This feeds real news content into your websites.

- Amazon.com Integration - Amazon sells thousands of products and services and you can now integrate these products into your new Directory Generator sites with a simple copy and paste mechanism. If you can **copy and paste** you can instantly start making extra revenue from Amazon.

- Google AdSense Integration – Since it's what this book is about, it's great that Directory Generator has an easy way for you to integrate Google's AdSense into your directory.

- Google Websearch Integration - Google recently released an add-on for AdSense that is called Websearch. It allows you to put a Google search box on your site and get paid for any AdSense click it creates. Now this feature is in Directory Generator.

- Built In Classified Ads - Making a directory is not enough. You need to be able to funnel the traffic to where you want. So the DG people created a way to for you to create Classified Ads in Directory Generator that let you promote and drive targeted traffic to any site you want, even if it is an affiliate program.

- Step Creation Wizard – Makes it easy to create DG pages. 8 simple steps, it's done. Seriously, you can probably complete the whole process in just a few minutes. Can be done by an 8-year-old.

- Pre-Made Templates – OK, so not everyone's a webmaster and you don't have to be one to make money with Google AdSense and DG with this feature. There are pre-made templates for you to use. Just select one, fill some stuff in, you're done.

DG also features PR Maximizer, which lets you search and find relevant and high quality sites for you to exchange links with. This software does all the work automatically for you, including telling you the site's PR, PageRank before you even contact them to talk about trading links.

PR Maximizer's output looks like this:

9.2 *Traffic TurboCharger*

Traffic TurboCharger (TTC) www.TrafficTurboCharger.com advertises itself as a "next generation SEO software" tool. Their biggest claim is that they optimize RSS feeds. The good things about having RSS feeds are:

- RSS feeds provide dynamically changing content so that every time the spiders come crawling to you page, it has new content. They really like that.

- RSS feeds give you instant theme-related content. Google, in particular, really loves this.

- RSS feeds provide content that is readable by search engines because the content is part of your page, unlike JavaScript feeds which offer no advantage because the little spiderbots can't read them.

- Your pages get indexed faster, since your content

changes daily, so you get more visits from the Googlebot. That's a very good thing.

One of the big advantages of RSS feeds is that you get content that looks like it's yours. You don't have to create it or pay a writer to write it. Best of all, you won't get in trouble with the search engines. Why not? Because RSS feeds are completely legitimate from the point of view of search engines.

They're also useful to your visitors, who are looking for information related to the theme of your site. And with RSS feeds, your site is constantly updated and fresh, because the feeds update as soon as new articles or content is added to the source you pull your content from. With big sources, this can happen every single hour.

Better yet, RSS feeds are completely automated so you don't have to do anything to keep your pages fresh and updated.

Chapter 10: The Eyes Have it—So Where are They?

When you're running a website, whoever is surfing it is staring at the screen...but where? One of the biggest questions for website designers is, "Where are the user's eyes looking?" Where do your eyes go when you read articles on the Web? What do you notice and what do you miss?

Well, we've got some answers for you, because this topic has been studied. Turns out that the upper left quarter of the screen gets the most attention, according to the Eyetrack III research of The Poynter Institute, the Estlow Center for Journalism & New Media, and Eyetools. But that's not all. There's more to it than that.

People's eyes have some very

common behavior patterns. It probably has to do with our hunter-gatherer ancestry.

First, we do reconnaissance, or "recon" as the military calls it. Users' eyes flick over the entire screen at whatever draws their attention. And what draws it most? Well, the first hot spots are headlines, photo captions, subheadings, links, menu items and the logo on the page—doesn't matter if it's a good logo or a bad one, people look at logos.

Then the upper left corner of the screen gets special attention, probably because that's where people expect to find the very best stuff. And the right-hand and lower part of the page almost always gets less attention.

This is info that site developers must

know: when you put your most important, vital content outside that critical upper left corner, that important content might as well be invisible when people are making the big decision: whether to stay on your site and read more or go somewhere else.

Yes, people scan a page quickly. But scanning has a purpose: it quickly identifies to a user what they really want to read. The good news is that if you can hook them right off the bat, when they start actually reading a news story on the Web, they read a larger proportion than if they were reading that very same story in the newspaper.

10.1 *Frontloading*

Frontloading means that you start headlines, paragraphs and links with the most important words. The first words should communicate the subject of the headline, paragraph or link. This is not like writing a novel or a story, where you have time to be coy and not get to the point for awhile. You've got about a quarter of a second to grab that user's attention or he won't read the rest of the sentence. Make the most of that opportunity.

If you do this, and you frontload your writing, especially at the top of the page, user's eyes will easily catch the most important info, and they'll keep reading.

Here are some examples of good frontloading:

- Foo Fighters release new cd
- Barbeque beef ribs recipes everyone will like
- Tom Cruise stars in a new movie

Here are some bad examples that are not frontloaded:

- New cd is being released, it's by the Foo Fighters
- Everyone will love these great new recipes for barbeque beef ribs
- New movie is coming out and it'll star Tom Cruise

10.2 Don't Nest, Just List

Remember back in school when the teacher asked you to make an outline and you went nuts making all sorts of nested sub-headings that looked like this?

1. The United States
   a. Texas
      i. Austin
         1. South Austin
            a. The 78704 zip

Don't do that.

Why? Because the last few items could be out of sight for many people when they skim-read. A straight margin is a whole lot easier to scan quickly on the

Web.

Nested dot-points and numbers are often used in business and government policy documents and management plans, and you're not making those, you're just writing content. Find another way to show the hierarchy of ideas. Web users do not like to try to read through a whole bunch of indentations, and you will lose some people before they even start reading.

10.3 Put web links where people will see them

If you're putting web links in, make sure they're where people will see them— not in that bottom right-hand Corner of Death! Yes, people notice links in web content. They're usually bright blue and underlined, so people notice them. Many people even read links before they look at headlines.

Now that you know that, make it easy for them to get to your links by consistently presenting them in list form or by slamming them right up against the left-hand margin.

Don't put your links in a sentence or they might end up in the invisible right-hand area of the content. Yes, this means you can't use the old "click here" convention, but for a good reason: it never worked very well anyway.

Here's an example of a good way to put in links:

"There are several cool skateboarding sites you might want to check out. They really rock and they've got some great gear you can pick up for not a lot of bucks.

Skateboard.com

Skatefreak.net

Liv2skat.biz

Here's an example of a bad way to use links:

If you want to read about the latest in cool tricks, check out skateboard.com. For the lowdown on which pro skaters are doing what and dating who, you want to see skatefreak.net. And one of my very favorite places to read blog is *liv2skat.com*.

10.4 *Never Hide Headers*

Remember how I said people look to the upper left? If you've been centering

132

your headlines and subheadings, do you still think that's a good idea? Well, it's not. Yeah, I know newspapers, magazines and books do it. So do lots of other sites. But that's just not where people want to look first.

They've tested this. Believe it or not, about 10-20 percent of people just literally do not see centered headlines, particularly if they're in a hurry (and who isn't these days?) They look in the top left hand corner of the content. And when they do, they see empty space, because the centered headline starts off to the right.

So what do they do? Instead of scanning right, they move their eyes down. And they miss the headlines.

Centered headlines are wasted headlines. If you center them, you've hidden them from 10-20% of your readers. Might as well not have them at all. And don't even think about right-justifying them.

Just left-justify them and don't ever worry about it again!

A word about tables: the ideal table for online is short, narrow, and only used for data. When a table is too wide or too long, part of it is out of the reader's natural field of vision. When they scan fast, they won't see all of it.

10.5 *Maximize your Click-Throughs with Placement*

Yeah, size matters, but so does placement...particularly as far as Google AdSense ads are concerned. Remember how I said to use the skyscraper format for ads, putting them in the margins as opposed to banner ads across the top or bottom?

Well, guess how much difference that can make. Go on, guess. OK, I'll tell you. Poorly placed ads, such as banner ads down at the very bottom of the page, might have a click-through rate of about 2.3% on a good day.

But well-placed ads, such as a nice skyscraper ad in that critical upper-left quadrant we talked about, can have a click-through rate as high as 40%.

And that's for the same ad. Yes, the very same ad can have a click-through rate of an abysmal 2.3% or an awesome 40%. It has nothing to do with the ad itself and everything to do with where you put it.

Another neat trick to maximize click-through is to massage the colors of the ads so that they fit in with the colors of your site. Ads that are seen as "fitting in" get more clicks than ads that clash.

The Ultimate AdSense Bible

Chapter 11: Building a Virtual Content Empire to Display Ads On

So now you're ready to build your content-rich empire and start raking in the bucks, right? Sure you are! You don't have to be a great writer, you just have to know where to get good writing. And heck, it really doesn't even have to be great. Just good.

Here are the steps you'll want to take:

1. Pick a domain name – this requires some thought, since even though it's not as critical

as it used to be to have a catchy domain name, it still matters to some users. Once you've picked one, check with http://www.web.com, or http://www.whois.net to see if it's available. If your favorite choice isn't available in .com format, consider being flexible and having it in .net, .biz, .org, or some other form.

2. Reserve the domain name. Web.com and many, many others offer that service.

3. Get web hosting. You'll want to shop around on

this one, since prices and services and terms & conditions vary greatly.

4. Set up your new domain, including your e-mail addresses.

5. Design your site, and start building pages.

6. Get some content. If you don't want to write it yourself, check out:

   ▪ http://www.ezinea rticles.com

   ▪ http://www.goartic les.com

   ▪ http://www.freshc ontent.net/

   ▪ http://www.elance. com to hire a

freelance writer who will write articles for you. Browse project postings first to see what other people usually ask for these articles—they are very popular.

- ArticleSiteBuilder.com builds your article sites automatically!

7. For good RSS feeds, check out:

- http://www.rsscontentbuilder.com/
- http://www.feedster.com/

8. Sign up with Google AdSense

9. Update content at least weekly

10. Go to mailbox, get checks.

11.1 *Blogging*

"Blog" is internet shorthand for "web log." They're like online diaries. Unlike a real diary, however, the entire world gets to read them.

You should seriously look into keeping a blog, or inviting others to blog on your site. Blogging is one of the hottest new forms of contents, and many readers find it positively addictive. In fact, it's grown so fast that many traditional news sources such as newspapers and TV stations are seeing an increase in declining readers and viewers (it was already declining due to the internet, but it got worse) because users are finding out they can go online and read a reporter's personal blog, which often gives juicy details that are not reported in formal news stories.

So people seek out blogs to get the real scoop. What does that mean for you? It means you should capitalize on it.

An easy way to start getting experience with writing a blog, before you get yours up and running, is to go to http://www.blogger.com and set up a practice blog.

11.2 *Blog and Ping—not just funny names*

Some of the very biggest buzz words on the internet right now are Blogging and Pinging. Many internet gurus claim these are the essentials for attracting visitors to your site and consequentially making those bucks through AdSense.

The best kind of blog lets readers put in their 2 cents worth. People love to be able to voice their opinions, and tend to get frustrated when they can't. Thus, the best blog is an online discussion web site that allows both you the web owner and your readers to voice their opinions on a specific subject.

So where do you begin? Well, for one thing, your blog needs to be specific to succeed, unless you're a celebrity. People will go to Paris Hilton's site to read just about any fool thing she writes off the top of her head, but don't think you can do that. I know it's not fair, but that's how it is.

If you're not famous, you need to focus on a niche topic. For instance rather than run a Blog on dogs why not specialize in black labs or some other breed? I guarantee you, if you put a cute picture of a black lab with a red bandana around her neck up, you'll have all the other black lab owners dropping by to tell stories about their own dogs.

Pinging, is how you tell the entire Blog community as a whole that your Blog site is up and running. Most Blog software has a feature that does this for you when a new post or comment has been made.

To put Blog software on your own

server and running it independently on your site, I have found Wordpress to be excellent software and this can be downloaded at http://www.wordpress.org

The Ultimate AdSense Bible

Chapter 12: Using RSS Feeds for Content

We live in the information age, and there's just no getting around it. Information and news happens every single day, and savvy site surfers will expect you to update your content regularly. In fact, they'd prefer you to do that daily, or even hourly. And yes—I mean 24/7 hours.

But you gotta sleep, right? And have some time off occasionally. So instead of spending every waking hour relentlessly surfing around from site to site looking for content, wouldn't you prefer it to be streamed in to your site? Well now you can, thanks to a very clever service, RSS.

RSS works so well that a lot of site owners swear it stands for 'Really Simple Syndication'. Why is it simple? Because you just select the content you like and have it delivered directly to your site.

If you're a busy person—and who isn't, these days—RSS feeds can take the hassle out of staying up-to-date, by streaming in the very latest information that you are interested in.

So where do you get this good stuff? Well, if it's news you want, most of the major news sites provide it since it is growing rapidly in popularity. A few news services that provide it are Guardian, New York Times and CNN.

12.1 *How do I start using RSS feeds?*

Well, the first thing you're gonna need is a news reader. There are many different versions of these, some of which are accessed using a browser, and some of which are downloadable applications. All allow you to display and subscribe to the RSS feeds you want.

My top picks for news readers, listed by the operating system they work with, are:

1. **Mac OS X: <u>NetNewsWire</u>**
   This is a simple yet elegant Mac-like aggregator that any one can use, yet it's powerful.

2. **Windows:** **<u>SharpReader</u>**
A very simple tool, but it delivers the goods.

3. **Linux: <u>Straw</u>** The best very aggregator for GNOME.

4. **Web: <u>Bloglines</u>** Enough said.

Now, after you've chosen a news reader, all you have to do is to decide what content you want. For example, if you would like the latest BBC News Entertainment stories, simply visit the Entertainment section and you will notice an orange RSS button on the left hand side.

The RSS button typically looks like this example from the BBC (http://www.bbc.com) page:

If you click on the RSS button you can subscribe to the feed in various ways: you can either drag the URL of the RSS feed into your news reader, or you can cut and paste the URL into a new feed in your news reader.

Some browsers, including Firefox, Opera and Safari, have functionality that automatically picks up RSS feeds for you. To make absolutely sure, check the details on the homesites of those browsers.

RSS feeds are a great way to get free content streaming onto your pages.

The only downside is that most of the free RSS feeds are news-oriented or entertainment-oriented, so if you run, say, a site that focuses on the latest video games, your audience may not really care that they can get the latest news streaming in there.

As far as the nitty-gritty, each RSS channel can contain up to 15 items and is easily parsed using Perl or other open source software. If you want more details, But you don't really have to worry too much over the details, since a simple Google search on "free open source RSS feed scripts" will produce the code you need to create your own RSS channel.

The next step, once you've created and validated your RSS text file, is to register it at the various aggregators, and start watching your traffic really spike. This happens because now any site can grab and display your feed regularly, which will drive traffic straight to your site.

It gets better—if you update your RSS file, all the external sites that subscribe to your feed will be automatically updated. What could be easier, other than watching those nice, fat checks from your Google AdSense ads roll in? Well, if you use RSS feeds, they'll work together!

The Ultimate AdSense Bible

Chapter 13: Summing Up

So that you will have them handy as a frame of reference, you'll want to bookmark the Google Guidelines for their search engine: http://www.google.com/webmasters/guidelines.html/

To get you on your way, here's a handy list of tips for using AdSense:

Making Money with AdSense -- Tip #1:
Start now!

It's as easy as falling off a log to generating revenue with Google AdSense. After you're accepted to the program, just add a few lines of html code to your site (Google shows you how once you're accepted) -- and voila!

Within a few minutes, your site will begin displaying AdWords, and so you can start making money. Each day you wait means you don't make the bucks you could. So start now.

Making Money with AdSense -- Tip #2:
Make content pages for your site -- and put AdWords on them.

Assuming your page is a decent one, the more pages you have displaying AdWords, the more money you'll earn.

If you already have a website, display AdWords on more pages.

157

And always, always, always focus on making more great content pages. I suggest that you budget time each week for creating pages (and sites) on topics you love. You'll find more on creating AdSense content pages in Tip #8.

And it's especially good if these content pages are very clearly focused. Then, Google will be able to serve highly relevant AdWords to your users. This means your visitors will be more interested in the ads, which results in higher click through rates -- and more money for you!

Making Money with AdSense -- Tip #3:
Whenever you can, use higher paying

keywords.

Obviously, you'll earn more if the average AdWord that Google displays pays more per click.

The question is: how do you get Google to display higher paying keywords?

Well, for one thing, don't get greedy and create pages on unrelated keywords just because they pay more. In other words, don't create a page on 'cell phone plans' on your motorcycle tire site just because 'cell phone plans' pays more than 'motorcycle tires.'

How to find out which keywords pay best? If you're a Google AdWords advertiser, you can log into your AdWords account and experiment.

If you're not an AdWords advertiser, use a free tool at the pay-per-click search engine, Overture.

Overture's tool lets you see what advertisers are paying on Overture for each keyword. Sure, Overture and Google don't pay the same. But they're not all that different, and this tool can give you a general idea of which keywords will pay more than others.

(Also, don't' forget Google's commission, so you have to allow for their cut on the amount an advertiser pays for each click.)

Making Money with AdSense -- Tip #4:
You want to make new pages with higher paying keywords (while keeping it real and relevant).

Sometimes, selecting different keywords on the same topic can really make a difference in earnings.

Pretend you have a gardening site and you want to create some new pages.

By carefully selecting which topics to focus on first, you can dramatically increase your income.

With the Overture tool mentioned

above, you can find out that 'water gardening' currently has a maximum price of $0.50, while 'gardening zone' is only $0.05. That means you can earn 10 times more by creating a page on 'water gardening' than 'gardening zones'! Which one to choose...yeah, that's tough!

What you want to do is use information to decide which relevant keywords to focus on as you go through the process of making new pages for your site.

Making Money with AdSense -- Tip #5:
Build a new site on high paying keywords.

This is one of my most lucrative pieces

of advice: create a brand new site to take advantage of Google AdSense by deliberately selecting a topic with high paying keywords.

Then, of course, you deliver dynamite content on that topic.

But how do you know what the highest paying keywords are?

Another tool you can use comes from pay-per-click search engine, 7Search. 7Search has a page on the **100 highest paying keywords**. Unfortunately, it's not perfect. The tool often 'times out' and gives you an error when you try to access the page. My best advice is just be patient and try several times to get this list—it's worth it.

Making Money with AdSense -- Tip #6:
Pull in qualified traffic to your site.

Basic marketing 101 says if you get more qualified visitors to your site, more people will naturally click on the displayed AdWords, and you'll earn more.

If you go back and read the chapters 6, 7, 8, & 9, you'll find some dynamite info.

Making Money with AdSense -- Tip #7:
Think about segmenting your sites: making some pages for high search engine traffic, other pages to sell

products, and still other pages just for Google AdSense.

To implement this, you'll need to recognize that different pages on your site can have different purposes. You may have pages designed to sell specific products. Others may be designed to rank high in the search engines (but don't ever try to trick the search engines). Still others can be designed for Google AdSense.

Now, once you know which pages you're creating for AdSense, your job is simple; select an appropriate keyword (or key phrase).

Then you'll use that keyword as the file name and put dashes between the words.

In the example above, you would use the file name 'water-gardening.html' for your water gardening page.

Best case scenario is that you're able to select keywords that are the highest paying keyword on the topic. By tweaking the file name, you may be able to improve your AdSense results dramatically.

Making Money with AdSense -- Tip #8:
Knock yourself out to make high quality information pages.

The ideal Google AdSense page should have great content about a very specific topic. Take pains to be very clear about what the topic is, and carefully choose the keyword (or key phrase) describing the topic. Users don't like vague pages that don't make it very clear what the page is all about.

Don't even think about trying to 'trick' AdSense. (I talked about that earlier, remember? They have penalties, including getting kicked out.) Don't create a page on one topic and give it a file name about a different topic—that's too confusing.

In a nutshell, you want to make sure the page you create offers great value to people interested in the topic. When you provide excellent information on a specific topic, your visitors will benefit and will be more likely to click through to relevant AdWords.

Making Money with AdSense -- Tip #9:
Select vertical AdWords format.

Everyone's seen way too many horizontal banner ads up top. Thus, Google recommends you choose the vertical -- not horizontal -- format to display your AdWords.   I agree. People have become "banner blind" to a horizontal format. Plus, Google has "trained" us to click on relevant text ads on their own site and they use the vertical format.

Making Money with AdSense -- Tip #10:
Make sure you display AdWords prominently.

It's to your financial advantage to put the AdWords near the top of your page on the right. Make sure there is enough "breathing room" -- i.e. white space around the ads -- so that they will easily attract your visitors.

Making Money with AdSense -- Tip #11:
Just don't do it--don't cheat.

I know it's tempting, because it seems so easy and it's just sitting there waiting for you to do it, but do not click on the AdWords displayed on your own site to increase your revenue. Google (rightfully) frowns on this.

Plus, Google has some of the smartest engineers around, and they are very good at detecting this kind of fraud. And really, for an extra $1, is it worth getting kicked out of a money-maker like AdSense? I think not...

In closing, I want to say that these strategies can help you maximize your revenue from Google AdSense. And I personally guarantee that you'll have a whole lot of fun creating content pages on topics you have a passion for.

So what're you waiting for? Go to Google AdSense right now, and start getting those revenue checks!

www.ingramcontent.com/pod-product-compliance
Lightning Source LLC
Chambersburg PA
CBHW052146070326
40689CB00050B/2142